UNSHAKABLE
YOU

5 Choices of
Emotionally Healthy People

John Opalewski

Unshakable You: 5 Choices of Emotionally Healthy People
ISBN 978-0-9890546-2-1
Copyright © 2015 by John Opalewski
Published by Converge Coaching, LLC, Washington, MI
Email: john@convergecoach.com
Website: www.convergecoach.com

Text & Cover Design: Keigh Cox

ACKNOWLEDGEMENTS

Writing a book is like building a house. You need blueprints, rough-in and finish workers, and a design landscaper for curb appeal. God has provided me with a talented set of builders.

First of all, thank you to my wife, Laura. You are my best friend, and a true gift from God. I appreciate your help with the rough-in phase.

A special shout-out to my sons Aaron, Andrew, Nathan, and Chad. I love each one of you deeply, and value your friendship.

Many thanks to my pastor, Aaron Hlavin, for your creative help with the blueprints, and for your ongoing belief in me.

Much gratitude to Janet Blakely for your expert assistance with editing the manuscript. You are a great finish worker.

Thanks also to Keigh Cox for bringing curb appeal with your graphic art and layout skills.

Many thanks to my Life Group family. Your prayers, encouragement, and friendship are priceless.

Last, but certainly not least, I am grateful to God for shepherding me through the extreme trial of depression, and using the experience to bring hope and healing to many. Only He can do that. *"Unless the Lord builds the house, its builders labor in vain"* Psalm 127:1.

CONTENTS

FOREWORD

I am honored to write the foreword to John Opalewski's newest book! I am grateful for the contribution John has made in *Unshakable You: 5 Choices of Emotionally Healthy People* because he hits the nail on the head in addressing one of the most and least talked about subjects—depression. Talk about depression is commonly discussed among people today, except among Christians—and especially Christian leaders. It's time we get comfortable talking about depression because, regardless of our status, our profession, or our spirituality, the negative effects of depression can be seen in lives, homes, churches, and organizations throughout the world.

In his preface, John states something many people don't realize: "Depression is highly preventable." Having experienced a season of clinical depression in my own life, after proper reflection, I was able to identify several contributing factors—each of which was preventable had I understood and applied the principles and practical exercises John outlines in *Unshakable You*.

The era of time in which we live is unquestionably the most exciting in all of history—but excitement has its price. Our fast-paced lives, without proper recovery, can lead not only to depleted energies but also to depressed emotions. And because the world is not going to slow down, it is all the more important a book like this be required reading for anyone who is attempting to do great things in life and great things for God. Even when our motives are pure in doing great things, without understanding the subtle encroachment of depression, even the most spiritual among us can succumb to emotionally unhealthy practices and outcomes.

One of my new practices in staying emotionally healthy is to regularly rehearse the five practical choices John outlines in *Unshakable You*. As a Vice President in a Christian University, I have now dedicated my life to investing into the next generation of Christian leaders and these five practical choices will now be a part of my leadership curriculum. Every person, every Christian, and every spiritual leader will benefit from reading *Unshakable You*.

Douglas M. Graham, D.Min.
Vice President of Spiritual Life
North Central University
Minneapolis, Minnesota

Unshakable You: 5 Choices of Emotional Healthy People
john@convergecoach.com

INTRODUCTION

The loud blast of a car horn filled the air . . . dad was waiting for us to pile in the station wagon once again for our weekly trek to church. It was 6:50 a.m. Sunday, and a herd of bleary-eyed kids stumbled into the car for the weekly ritual of Mass. Forty-five minutes of going through the motions at church completed my religious duties and I could forget about God until next Sunday.

As I grew older, I noticed a disconnect between what happened on Sunday at church and what happened the rest of the week. My faith was not integrated into how I talked, behaved, and treated others. I found God to be distant and almost unreachable. Going to church became a mind-numbing exercise.

As a teenager, this disconnect grew into a search for fulfillment. I tried alcohol and other drugs for a while, thinking this would make me happy. Yet with the passing of every party, I felt emptier on the inside. On several occasions I remember staggering across the doorstep to my home and thinking, "there has to be more to life than this."

Enter my friend who lived across the street—Kirk. He had invited me to his church on several occasions, and I accepted. I didn't always understand what the people at his church said, but they seemed excited about Jesus. On June 13, 1974, Kirk invited me to a Christian concert at a local coffeehouse. By this time, I knew what he was trying to do—get me "saved"—or in other words, convert me to Christ. I gave him reasons why I couldn't go, but he kept asking. Grudgingly, I agreed to go—but I remember saying to myself, "I'm not getting saved tonight."

At the end of the concert, an invitation to follow Jesus was given. Despite my planned resistance, I found myself wanting to respond. Frozen to my seat . . . I asked Jesus to come into my heart. Almost immediately, I felt as though a load of bricks had dropped from my shoulders. For the first time in my life, I felt clean on the inside. I sensed my old, empty life had ended . . . and a brand new chapter had begun.

Many things changed in the weeks to follow. My craving for alcohol and other drugs disappeared. Instead of emptiness, I felt joy, purpose, and a clear sense of direction. My party buddies definitely knew something was different. I shocked my friends when I eventually became courageous enough to tell them what happened.

Within one year of my conversion, I began to sense God calling me to some sort of ministry. I made a decision to attend Oral Roberts University for training. I graduated from ORU several years later, and was off to pursue my dream of changing the world for Jesus. But lurking in the shadows was a monster I had no idea existed. The spiritual excitement in my life masked an underlying lack of emotional health. In November 1992 everything changed.

At the time, I was the lead pastor of a growing church. Life seemed good at home and in the ministry. But for weeks during autumn 1992, I had trouble sleeping, and had no appetite. Waves of sadness overwhelmed me, but I had no idea why. Panic attacks and uncontrollable crying spells became common—it was terrifying and I didn't know what was happening to me. I was suicidal and contemplating the least painful way to end my life.

Fortunately, I had wise friends, a good medical doctor, and

a competent counselor who identified the problem. Clinical depression had brought my world to a crashing halt.

Up to that point, I had little room in my thinking for depression. It was something weak-minded people struggled with, not a mature Christian. After all, I had been walking with God for eighteen years. I had been a pastor for twelve years. The spiritual disciplines of Bible study, prayer, and Scripture memory were part of my daily routine. How could this happen to someone like me? In that dark moment, I felt as if God had betrayed me. But over time, I discovered depression happens to all kinds of people—even to some who love Jesus.

You may have a story like mine (you can't have mine—we all have a story). Maybe your dreams have been crushed under the heavy weight of depression. Perhaps its dark cloud has negatively colored your view of life. I want you to know there's hope for you. You won't be able to get better on your own—you'll need a team of professionals and friends. You'll have to unlearn dysfunctional thinking patterns and replace them with healthy ones. But you can get better. The following pages are dedicated to helping you recover.

Maybe you are reading this book and have no issues currently with depression. Be thankful to God for your health. But understand depression is easier to prevent than it is to cure. Educating yourself while healthy minimizes your future risk.

What I didn't understand back in 1992 was the pervasive nature of depression in our world—even in the church world. I somehow overlooked the depressive episodes of King David . . . one of Israel's greatest leaders . . . and the dark seasons experienced by the Old Testament prophets Elijah and Jeremiah, even though I read about them multiple times. I failed to recognize spiritual giants like Charles Spurgeon, Martin Luther, and John Calvin all suffered from this affliction.

One of the greatest presidents in our nation's history, Abraham Lincoln, battled with depression. In an article written by Joshua Wolf Schenk we read: "He (Lincoln) often wept in public and recited maudlin poetry. He told jokes and stories at odd times— he needed the laughs, he said, for his survival. As a young man he talked more than once of suicide, and as he grew older he said he saw the world as hard and grim, full of misery, made that way by fate and the forces of God. "No element of Mr. Lincoln's character," declared his colleague Henry Whitney, "was so marked, obvious and ingrained as his mysterious and profound melancholy." His law partner William Herndon said, "His melancholy dripped from him as he walked."[1]

In our generation, movie stars Robin Williams and Lee Thompson Young, football players Junior Seau and Jovan Belcher, WWF wrestlers Chris Benoit and Sean O'Haire, have ended their lives prematurely. According to the National Institute of Mental Health (NIMH), suicide is the fourth leading cause of death in the United States for adults ages 18 to 65.[2] Depression is indicated in 90% of suicides.[3]

The emotional experiences of these people we consider larger than life reveal depression is no respecter of persons. The number of people battling depression is staggering. Estimates range anywhere from 20 to 23 million people in the United States—and as many as 340 million worldwide, depending on the statistical source. At its current rate of increase, depression will be the number one health issue in the world by 2030. We are witnessing an emotional epidemic.

What causes this oppressive emotional condition? No single answer exists. Depression can be event-driven. It can collapse on top of you when suffering a major loss in your life. Depression can be incremental. It can result from years of improper mental and emotional behavior. It can issue from the cumulative impact of multiple sustained stresses pushing you over the edge emotionally. No matter the source, clinical depression is more than just a few bad days in a row. It is much deeper than simply "experiencing the blues."

Depression is no respecter of race, social status, gender, or religious persuasion. It affects Christians and non-Christians without prejudice. The awful truth is it can happen to anyone, even to people who love God. If you have not experienced the long dark tunnel of clinical depression, let me try to describe what it feels like.

1. Depression feels like you've plunged off a cliff into a black hole of sadness

It can engulf you to the degree you feel like an emotional zombie. Listen to the words of an anonymous depression survivor: "When I was depressed and I looked out my window, the landscape looked absolutely flat and colorless." In Matthew 26:38, Jesus told His friends in the Garden of Gethsemane, *"My soul is overwhelmed with sorrow to the point of death."* I am not saying Jesus was depressed, but His words capture the feeling. When you are depressed, you feel dead on the inside.

2. Depression is not something that responds to the sheer force of our will

Recovery is not merely a matter of pulling yourself up by your own bootstraps. You cannot smile your way out of it or somehow magically snap out of it. You cannot bargain your way out of depression. I remember negotiating with God while in the middle of the black hole—"Lord, if you get me out of this, I'll do whatever You want me to do." My hope was He would deliver me instantaneously. God had other plans.

3. Depression often rears up when least expected

Elizabeth Sherrill states: "The terror of depression, the dark mystery that distinguishes it from sorrow, is that it can cast its gray pall about us when the sun is the brightest."[4] In 1992, I had (and still have) a wonderful wife and four healthy boys. The church I served as pastor was enjoying excellent growth spiritually, numerically, and financially. Externally life was good, but internally I was an emotional train-wreck.

The professional counselor I sought out to help me get to the bottom of the depression opened my eyes to see the truth. And the truth was this emotional crisis that seemingly "came out of nowhere" in November 1992 had been building for years. The unique pressures of leading an organization forced to the surface my flawed approach to mental and emotional maturity. My total disregard for sensible scheduling and ignorance of how to handle difficult people finally caught up to me. And consequently, I found myself in the battle of my life, hanging on by a thread.

In John 10:10, Jesus said, *"I have come that they may have life and have it to the full."* My wife Laura and I are committed to helping people live a healthy, fulfilling, joy-filled, and fun life. We believe God intends for His people to have fullness in both their personal life as well as their careers.

DEPRESSION IS HIGHLY PREVENTABLE

This brings me to the reason for writing this book. Depression is highly preventable. And prevention is almost always easier (and more cost-effective) than recovery. I spend a fair amount of time teaching and preaching the message of emotional health in churches, leadership conferences, and training events. Scores of people in the business world have talked to me about their struggles with depression. The response to our message has been overwhelmingly positive from church attendees as well as their leaders—and from my friends in business.

The need for sound, practical, biblical teaching regarding emotional health has never been greater. The upcoming chapters are written out of the fires of my personal experience. It is my hope the content will help you prevent experiencing depression altogether, or shorten your recovery time if you are currently battling the affliction.

The chapters ahead introduce five practical choices lending to solid emotional health. Many emotionally healthy choices exist . . . but I've boiled them down to five main behaviors. I've dedicated a chapter to each one. These five action steps are not substitutes for medical help or therapeutic counseling, but they are part of a larger strategy to get well and/or stay well emotionally.

CHOICE 1
LOVE YOURSELF

Emotional health is a choice. If you choose to ignore your emotional health, no one else will pay attention to it for you. Nor should they, for you are responsible for this part of your life—not your spouse, your children, your boss, your friends, or your pastor. Even for those who suffer with bipolar

EMOTIONAL HEALTH IS A CHOICE

disorder or schizophrenia, options exist. I will give more detail on those two afflictions in chapter five. With this in mind, let's consider how you can take appropriate responsibility here.

The first choice—love yourself—lays a solid foundation for emotional health. Jesus stated in Matthew 22:37-40 the greatest commandment in the Bible is: " *'Love the Lord your God with all your heart and with all your soul and with all your mind.' This is the first and greatest commandment. And the second is like it: 'Love your neighbor as yourself.' All the Law and the Prophets hang on these two commandments.* " Let's make one thing clear: The five choices of emotionally healthy people assume you already possess a passionate, growing, relationship with Jesus Christ. Walking close to Him by reading and meditating on Scripture, and cultivating a private prayer and praise life provide the anchors for emotional fitness. In Psalm 62:6 David wrote: *"He alone is my rock and my salvation; He is my fortress, I will not be shaken."* If you are not a Jesus-follower yet, this book will still help you—but it's easier to implement these choices with His help.

Now you may be wondering: "How do I love myself without crossing over the line into selfishness?" Looking back to Matthew chapter 22, notice in verse 39 Jesus' use of the word, *"as."* It is the Greek connector word *"os"* and it means *"in the same manner as."* Jesus commanded us to love our neighbor in the same manner as we love ourselves. The most important command in the Bible is actually a three-parter: love God, love our neighbor, and love ourselves. Loving God is fairly easy for most Christians. Loving others . . . well, at least it's on our radar. Loving ourselves is where many of us go off the rails.

The concept of loving yourself is either unknown, misunderstood, ignored, or simply dismissed by many people. The question we need to consider is—why did Jesus put it in the top three? One reason may be He knew following His command in its entirety would give us the foundation for long-term emotional health. It would provide the basis for a fruitful life.

Let's consider several biblical *love-yourself* principles:

1. Healthy self-talk

This describes how I talk to myself about myself. Self-talk is not usually spoken out loud—more often it's a running conversation we have with ourselves internally. However, one morning I pulled into the work parking lot, only to find I had left my PC at home—major mistake when you work for a technology company. I distinctly remember saying *out loud*—"I am so stupid!"

That kind of negative inward conversation was a familiar pattern when I got stressed out. But on this specific morning, right on the heels of those words I felt a twinge of conviction telling me, "It is not right for you to say those words about yourself. I'm not going to let you get away with it anymore." I recognized the source of the twinge was the Holy Spirit.

Let me ask some key questions: Do you talk to yourself in a self-critical way? If yes, do you understand the damage inflicted when you talk to yourself harshly? Proverbs 18:21 teaches us: *"The tongue has the power of life and death, and those who love it will eat its fruit."* Simply put, our words carry great power. God used words to create the universe. They have the power to create or destroy, heal or wound.

> OUR WORDS CARRY GREAT POWER

Nobody talks to you more than you talk to yourself. Verbally assaulting yourself damages your emotional health—every time. Being kind to yourself with words enhances your emotional health—every time. Ephesians 4:15 tells us *"...[S]peaking the truth in love, we will in all things grow up . . ."* This includes telling the truth in love to yourself.

Loving yourself means you gain increasing control of your self-talk. It requires you to learn to speak to yourself with kindness—to treat yourself as well as you treat others.

2. Authentic humility

Humility is sometimes confused with thinking negatively about yourself, or minimizing your gifts. Some of us think being down-to-earth means we let ourselves be a doormat for people to step on and treat poorly. These self-defeating behaviors do not equal authentic humility.

Mother Teresa stated: "Humility is the mother of all virtues, because you know what you are." In Romans 12:3 the apostle

Paul tells us: *"For by the grace given me I say to every one of you: Do not think of yourself more highly than you ought, but rather think of yourself with sober judgment, in accordance with the measure of faith God has given you."* We often misinterpret Paul's words here to mean we should think lowly of ourselves. He never said that. The phrase *"sober judgment"* comes from the Greek word *"sopron"* and it means *"to be in one's right mind,"* or to think correctly.

If you read the verses following in Romans 12, Paul gives a short teaching on spiritual gifts. It seems clear in this context Paul's intent in verse three was to explain biblical humility as an accurate grasp of our strengths and weaknesses. A humble person possesses a well-balanced, honest evaluation of himself. Don't confuse this wonderful character trait with verbally abusing yourself or allowing others to beat you up with their words.

3. Understand the difference between loving yourself and self-centeredness

Jesus' command to love your neighbor as yourself was not a commercial for selfishness. This would contradict His words in Luke 9:23 stating, *"If anyone would come after me, he must deny himself…"*

I love how the Bible clarifies these seeming contradictions. Acts 20:28 helps us understand how both ideas in Matthew 22 and Luke 9 come together. Allow me to set the scene: In Acts 20 the apostle Paul was delivering his final farewell to the Ephesian elders. He told them he would never see them again, and in this emotional moment he commanded them in verse 28 to *"Keep watch over yourselves and all the flock of which the Holy Spirit has made you overseers."*

The phrase *"keep watch"* comes from the Greek word *"prosecete"* which means *"to attend to, to guard, to pay attention to, to devote thought and effort to.* " Paul's final farewell to his friends included a command to attend to themselves and the flock—pay attention to themselves *and* the flock—devote thought and effort to themselves and the flock. We get into emotional trouble when we do only one of these.

If all you do is focus on yourself, you'll shrivel up and die. If all you do is concentrate on others, you'll shrivel up and die. When we piece together these verses in Matthew 22, Luke 9, and Acts 20, we discover loving yourself includes paying attention to yourself while at the same time caring about others. Self-centeredness is focusing exclusively on yourself. Philippians 2:4 confirms this idea: *"Each of you should look not only to your own interests, but also to the interests of others."* Notice Paul's choice of words here: *"Not only"* and *"also."* He didn't say, "Don't look to your own interests" nor "Look only to others' interests." He said, "Look to your own stuff—but also look to others' stuff. Paul was not making an *either-or* argument—it was a *both-and* statement.

4. Embrace God's opinion of you

Self-image gets a bad rap in many Christian circles. Psalm 139:1-3 helps us think the right way about self. *"O LORD, you have searched me and you know me. You know when I sit and when I rise; you perceive my thoughts from afar. You discern my going out and my lying down; you are familiar with all my ways."*

Loosely translated, these first three verses tell us God sees past our exterior and into our private thoughts, attitudes, and motives. Kind of scary, isn't it? He knows everything about us—the good, the bad, and the ugly. Yet the Bible makes it clear: He loves us anyway. He places high value on everyone.

David continued in verses 13-14, *"For you created my inmost being; you knit me together in my mother's womb. I praise you because I am fearfully and wonderfully made; your works are wonderful, I know that full well."* David was aware of and impressed with how skillfully God put him together. Some of us need to tape on our mirror the phrase *"I am fearfully and wonderfully made"* and say it out loud every morning. Why, you ask? Because it's true.

WE'RE NEVER OUTSIDE OF GOD'S THOUGHTS

He added in verses 17-18, *"How precious to me (concerning me) are your thoughts, O God! How vast is the sum of them! Were I to count them, they would outnumber the grains of sand."* How many grains of sand are there on a beach or in a desert? They are innumerable. Verses 17-18 reveal the same God who created the universe thinks about us all the time. We are never outside of His thoughts. Ponder this truth for a moment and be amazed. Loving ourselves means we embrace the truth that we are the *"...apple of God's eye"* (Deuteronomy 32:10). Someone has said: *"If you put a low value on yourself, rest assured nobody else will raise your price."*

5. Get in touch with your soul

Proverbs 19:8 tells us, *"He who gets wisdom loves his own soul."* For some people, the idea of paying attention to their soul—the mental, emotional, and "will" part of their being—is a new thought. Unfortunately, what you don't know about this component of your humanity can hurt you.

The need for this kind of wisdom came home to me in November 1992. I mentioned my depressive episode in this book's introduction, but allow me to give you more detail. Since the earliest days of my walk with God, I understood the parts of the great commandment related to loving Him and people. I was clueless when it came to the part about loving myself. Up to that point it never occurred to me to take care of myself emotionally. And I discovered a lack of Proverbs 19:8 wisdom was a formula which often ends in emotional disaster. My ignorance of the love-yourself principle eventually caught up with me. Several extremely stressful events all hit at the same time and brought my emotional crisis to the forefront.

The symptoms included:

1. Little sleep for an extended period of time
Here was a typical night: I would anxiously lie wide awake in bed until 1:00 a.m., finally drift off to sleep for an hour, and then wake up around 2:00 a.m. and remain awake for the rest of the night. This disturbed sleep pattern lingered for weeks.

2. Little-to-no appetite
Not wanting to eat should have been an obvious warning flag something was seriously wrong with me. I come from a family of big eaters. At holiday gatherings, our family took more pictures of the food than people.

3. Anxiety, overwhelming sadness, and an incredibly deep awareness of emotional pain
It was like a thick, black emotional fog rolled into my thoughts and feelings, accompanied by the sincere belief my life was truly over. I began to think about the least painful way to kill myself.

Compounding the problem, I didn't know what was happening to me. I thank God often for the wise family, friends, and medical professionals who identified it as clinical depression. It was a small bit of comfort to at least have a name for my distress, and to understand I was not the only one in the world facing the long dark tunnel.

BE NICE TO YOURSELF

Recovery from this crisis didn't happen overnight. Recuperating from depression felt like a gradual resurrection from the dead. It was a lengthy, difficult process which started with understanding these verses in Matthew 22 and Acts 20. I needed the assistance of a professional counselor for a short time. The first thing he told me was, "John, you need to learn to be nice to yourself." I didn't understand what he was telling me in the moment . . . but he was simply reiterating my need to obey the third part of the Greatest Commandment—"love yourself."

Loving yourself this way takes practice to implement. It often requires the help of a qualified counselor, a mentor, a life coach, or a close friend who is living the concept already. Regardless of how much effort it takes, obeying all three parts of the Greatest Commandment provides a solid foundation for long-term emotional health, as well as sustainable success in your family and career.

Pause a moment and say out loud the following *I-CHOOSE* statement:

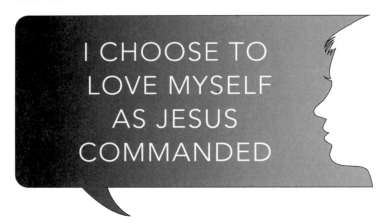

CHOICE 2
MANAGE YOUR ANGER

A husband remarked to his wife one day, "When I get mad at you, you never fight back. How do you control your anger? His wife replied, "I clean the toilet bowl." "How does that help?" her husband asked. She smiled and replied, "I use your toothbrush!" (Some of you may suddenly have the urge to run and buy a new stash of toothbrushes—just in case!)

Emotionally healthy people learn how to manage their anger. In Ephesians 4:26 the apostle Paul wrote: *"In your anger do not sin."* Six simple words, if obeyed, would drastically improve our lives both individually and corporately.

Unfortunately, anger often fools us. It is a tricky emotion. Some Christians have been taught it is a sin to get angry. In reality, the slow burn is a neutral emotion. It's what we do with it that makes the difference. Experience teaches us it's easier to sin when we are mad. We often say something we should not say or do something we should not do when upset.

Anger can be expressed outwardly or submerged inwardly. It's fairly easy to identify rage expressed outwardly. Many of you observe this variety during your daily commute to work. Anger submerged inwardly is more subtle—but it is corrosive to our health. Repression often results in

REPRESSION OFTEN RESULTS IN DEPRESSION

depression. Some experts have even described depression as anger turned inward. If this is true, we need to get a handle on this emotion because life presents numerous opportunities for irritations to occur.

Unfortunately, many people simply do not know how to process their anger. This is one reason devoted Christians suffer from depression in significant numbers. Many Jesus-followers are afraid to even admit they occasionally get irate. The idea Christians are exempt from normal human emotions is silly. We get angry. Denying it is not an appropriate response. Neither is blowing our top. Expressing it in a healthy manner without sinning is a more mature reaction. Responding this way is an important choice we make in constructing a healthy emotional life.

With this in mind, how do you get a handle on your anger? How do you manage your temper? Consider the following steps:

1. Conduct an honest appraisal

This includes understanding:

a. Anger is part of the human experience

It happens when someone violates you or crosses a healthy boundary you have established. In these situations, anger is simply part of being human.

b. Anger often involves emotional residue

Several years ago I experienced severe pain in the middle of my back. After consulting with a chiropractor, I learned the source of my back pain was a compressed vertebra in my neck. Once the chiropractor addressed my neck issue, the back pain subsided.

Likewise, the present occasion for our anger may not

be the real reason we are annoyed, frustrated, or outraged. Usually something is brewing just beneath the surface, fueling these emotions. Emotional residue can include leftover feelings we have carried from a negative event in our past. It can center around a rough day at the office which sometimes translates to over-the-top reactions toward your spouse and children at home. Has a difficult evening at home ever contributed to a disproportionate reaction over a minor incident with your work colleagues the next day? Discovering what is boiling beneath the surface helps us to more accurately assess our anger.

Residual anger can run fairly deep. For example, if you were raised in a home where alcohol was abused, I'm guessing your home was full of rage. If you fail to work through the residual emotions associated with growing up in such a volatile environment, they will remain hidden, boiling just beneath the surface. If you are feeling the pressure of heavy financial debt, or the stress of being a perfectionist, it will not take much for the geyser to erupt.

c. Anger can sometimes be the right response

Appropriate occasions for anger can include, for example, when someone you love betrays you. If a person abuses you physically, it is normal to get mad. If he or she takes advantage of you mentally, emotionally, verbally, or spiritually, you should expect to feel negative emotions about it eventually. Anger is an appropriate response when you see injustice inflicted on others. With appropriate anger, the depth and duration of our anger is consistent with the depth and duration of the offense.

d. Anger can be holy

Jesus demonstrated holy anger on multiple occasions. *"Another time he went into the synagogue, and a man with a shriveled hand was there. Some of them were looking for a reason to accuse Jesus, so they watched him closely to see if he would heal him on the Sabbath. Jesus said to the man with the shriveled hand, 'Stand up in front of everyone.' Then Jesus asked them, 'Which is lawful on the Sabbath: to do good or to do evil, to save life or to kill?' But they remained silent. He looked around at them in anger and, deeply distressed at their stubborn hearts, said to the man, 'Stretch out your hand.' He stretched it out, and his hand was completely restored"* (Mark 3:1-5).

Why did Jesus get mad in this situation? Was it because He took the stubborn silence of those in the synagogue personally? Probably not. It's more likely He was upset because religious tradition was getting in the way of a man who needed healing.

Horrible events happen in the world that should result in holy anger. When children are abused, it should make us furious. When youngsters (or adults) are sex-trafficked, we should feel outraged. Holy anger has to do with the ultimate well-being of others.

e. Anger brings attention to root issues we need to address

I remember one summer morning when I was about twelve years old my dad assigned me one of my least favorite jobs—weeding his flower garden. Ugh. I wanted to hang out with my friends, play baseball, ring a few doorbells and run away. Pulling weeds was not my idea of a good time.

While in the garage reluctantly gathering the weed-pulling tools, I spotted a stack of eight fifty-pound bags of peat moss . . . and suddenly had an idea. I could accelerate the completion of my dreaded assignment. I took all eight bags of peat moss, poured them on top of the weeds and smoothed out the pile. Dad's flower garden never looked better. And within thirty minutes I was off to cause neighborhood mischief with my friends.

When dad returned in the evening, he glanced at my work and commended me on a job well-done. "Looks great, John," I remember him saying. Somehow he forgot about those bags in the garage. (Maybe having nine kids had something to do with his forgetting). What I didn't realize was the peat moss was actually *feeding* the weeds. My cover-up made the problem worse. Three days later, when the weeds started sticking up through the 400-pound layer of peat moss, dad's view of my work deteriorated considerably.

I don't know what your "peat moss" is when it comes to your anger. Maybe it is simply denying your irritable feelings instead of acknowledging them as possibly a *God-given* signal something in your life needs attention. Anger often exposes areas of our heart needing development. Can I encourage you to stop throwing dirt over your anger in an unwise attempt to cover it up? Let God show you the root so you can deal with it and get healthy.

ANGER IS A GOD-GIVEN SIGNAL THAT SOMETHING NEEDS ATTENTION

f. Anger can alert us to our limitations

If you find yourself increasingly irritable—pay attention. Could it be due to overscheduling? Maybe it is the result of encountering a string of emotionally-draining events with little-to-no-time-in-between for recuperation. Consider your anger as a possible indicator you are overcommitting your time and emotional resources.

Choosing to manage your anger requires an honest appraisal. This includes understanding the root of our anger so we can manage it effectively. It's better to cut it off at the source rather than cutting it off at the surface.

Once an honest appraisal is made, we get a better grip on our anger by doing some additional detective work. We uncover and let go of immature responses to our rage.

2. Identify and reject unhealthy expressions of anger

Here are three examples:

a. Caving in

Caving in looks like this: "Well, I'm an angry person because anger was modeled to me as a child! And besides, I'm (insert your nationality here), you know—it's genetic!" In this unhealthy response we throw up our hands in despair and give way to our rage. Even if we grew up in an emotionally volatile home, the good news is God can change these dysfunctional patterns if we are willing to cooperate with Him.

b. Blaming

Someone has written: *"To err is human—to blame it on somebody else is even more human."* Blaming sounds something like this: "I wouldn't act this way if you would just behave better!" Do we realize how lame those words sound? You are responsible to manage your anger. Assume ownership for it instead of blaming others.

YOU ARE
RESPONSIBLE
TO MANAGE
YOUR ANGER

c. Submerging

This expression involves shoving your anger underground. Submerged rage often leads to bitterness, the nursing of grudges, difficulty granting forgiveness, and eventually depression. You may be thinking, "John you don't know what that person did to me!" You're right—I don't. But an unwillingness to forgive keeps you chained to the person who hurt you. If the wound was severe, you'll need to work through some things—often with the help of a qualified counselor. The goal is to arrive at a place where forgiveness is possible. Remember, ultimately forgiving them frees *you*.

Forgiveness doesn't mean you forget the event(s) happened—or you trust the person again—it means you don't hold it against him anymore. More on forgiveness in the next step.

You do not want to cave in to your anger. You don't want to blame others for it. And you do not want to submerge it. So how does a person deal with this emotion in appropriate ways lending to emotional health? I wish I was batting a thousand when it comes to anger management, but I'm still a work-in-progress. I'm sure you can relate. Let's look at better ideas we can use in response.

3. Five ways to express anger properly

In Ephesians 4:31, the apostle Paul commanded his friends, *"Get rid of all bitterness, rage and anger . . ."* He was not instructing them to deny these emotions or pretend they didn't exist. He was encouraging his readers to deal with them. We do not get rid of our anger by pushing it down or pretending it is not there. We dispose of it by accepting responsibility for it and learning to express it appropriately. Let's consider five ways to apply Paul's instruction:

a. Understand the negative impact of mishandled anger

When we go ballistic it is destructive to ourselves and to those in the path of our rage. Mishandled anger leaves a trail of relational destruction in its wake. It has the ability to isolate us from the people who love us the most. While you may get over losing your temper rather quickly—those around you most likely will not.

b. Take a step back and identify its roots

When you feel anger rising, ask yourself: *"Why am I angry right now? What is ticking me off here, really?"* Ask God to show you any residual source fueling your rage. Talking with others who will reflect the truth back to you can help pinpoint the source.

c. Identify relationships or situations where an emotional eruption is more likely to occur

Do you have any of those? For me, it's getting ready to go on vacation. You know why? Because I like to leave for vacation on time. When we agree to leave at 8:00 a.m. for vacation . . . I'm very committed to 8:00 a.m. Thinking back, the family never really agreed on our vacation departure time. It was an agreement inside my head. No matter—I would get stressed out when we were fifteen minutes late leaving. I thank God for sending my wife and children to help me modify my vacation misbehavior.

I don't know what sets you off, but learn to identify situations and people tending to stress you ahead of time so you can spend additional minutes asking God for strength. You may need to fast and pray, depending on the circumstances.

d. Become committed to forgive no matter what

One of the hardest things to do in life is to forgive a person who has deeply wounded you. Forgiveness is not usually the first thing on our mind when we're hurt. We are more likely to nurse a grudge, become bitter, or plot our revenge.

Forgiveness doesn't diminish or marginalize the pain inflicted on us. It simply moves us toward healing. Resentment may initially feel good—even justified—but it keeps us chained to the person who hurt us.

> FORGIVENESS DOESN'T MARGINALIZE YOUR PAIN

The longer we live, and the more people we interact with, the more opportunities exist to practice mercy. When we think about this subject, it's easy to become confused. Some Christians have been shamed or bullied into forgiving. Rarely have they been taught how to release their offender.

Let's be honest. Most offenses that happen to us we

need to get over quickly. For example: a driver cuts you off on the freeway, a store clerk treats you rudely, a colleague rolls his eyes at your suggestions to improve the company, an acquaintance at church fails to notice you as he passes by in the hallway. Let minor violations such as these roll off your back and simply move on. Refuse to be easily offended.

But some wounds cut deep. King David wrote: *"If an enemy were insulting me, I could endure it; if a foe were raising himself against me, I could hide from him. But it is you, a man like myself, my companion, my close friend, with whom I once enjoyed sweet fellowship as we walked with the throng at the house of God"* (Psalm 55:12-14).

Can you feel the pain in David's words? He had been betrayed by a close friend. Deep relational injuries require some time and effort to work through. In deep-wound situations:

i. Be honest about the harm done

Real forgiveness is not possible without acknowledging the anger you feel about the offense and the resulting wound. In fact, some counselors believe you cannot fully pardon someone until you have acknowledged the pain he or she has caused you. Some of us jump the gun when it comes to releasing a person who hurt us as a coping mechanism to avoid the difficult work of processing our anger.

ii. Be committed to the process

Forgiveness isn't always instantaneous. In the Gospel of Matthew, Jesus said, *"For if you forgive men when they sin against you, your heavenly Father will also forgive you.*

But if you do not forgive men their sins, your Father will not forgive your sins" (Matthew 6:14-15). His words here often have been used as a sledgehammer to club each other into prematurely showing mercy. We end up mouthing the words "I forgive you," while our heart remains in an emotional rage. Jesus commands us to forgive—but occasionally we have to work through a process in order to release our offender. And depending on the severity of the wound, the process takes commensurate time.

If you have been betrayed by a close friend, or stabbed in the back by a family member, you'll need time just to figure out which way is up. You'll probably also need to reach out to qualified people who can legitimately help you work through your pain. Prayer is a huge part of the process as well.

iii. Be patient with yourself

In deep-wound circumstances, you may have buried the hatchet a while back, but occasionally something will trigger the memory of the wound and you feel anger again. If and when this occurs, do not despair. It does not mean the forgiveness you extended a while back wasn't valid—it just means there is more forgiving to do. Keep at it until the process is complete. You may wonder, "How do I know when I'm done?" This can be difficult to determine. All I can say is, if you no longer wish a slow, painful death on the offender, you're making progress.

Resentment and bitterness imprison us in our pain. Forgiveness propels us toward healing. So when you've been deeply hurt, and the opportunity to forgive presents itself: be honest about the injury, commit yourself to the process, and give yourself some grace as you work toward forgiveness. If the wound inflicted on you was severe, it will take time and effort to forgive . . . but ultimately, releasing your offender frees you. And it helps manage your anger.

e. Learn to be assertive rather than aggressive or passive

Aggression includes foul language, yelling, or getting physical with people. Passivity is another word for repression. Here we stuff our anger and let it boil on the inside. An example of passivity is giving someone the silent treatment.

Assertiveness, on the other hand, means standing up for yourself by expressing your needs to others with love and respect. It outlines how the behavior of the person violating you is negatively impacting your life. It acknowledges any contribution you yourself have made to the situation—but it doesn't excuse the other person's contribution either. Let me give you two examples of assertively expressing anger.

I currently work for an information technology company. One of my past roles included supporting sales executives from a technical design perspective. I remember one particular client meeting where the sales executive cut me off twice in the middle of making what was about to be (in my opinion) a brilliant point. I said nothing to him about this during the client meeting. Afterward in private, I mentioned the multiple interruptions to him and how it made me feel as though he didn't trust me to say the right thing. I told him I understood we had not worked together much—and consequently maybe he didn't trust me—but if we were going to work well together, he needed to let me talk in customer meetings. I braced myself for a negative reaction—but he was not defensive and he agreed. And from then on, our relationship has improved. The key here was being clear with my colleague about what my specific needs were in the situation without ripping his head off.

On another occasion, I had a direct report who consistently arrived late for work in our call center. Her peers were growing agitated about her tardiness because they ended up having to cover for her. Customers don't care if you're short-handed—they want their problems fixed. The team's discontent filtered back to me and I called the offender into my office. My conversation with her was brief: "It has come to my attention you have been consistently late to work over the past several weeks. Is that accurate?" "Pretty much," she responded. I was caught off guard by her honest response. I recovered quickly and asked "Are you having problems with your car that are preventing you from arriving on time?" "Nope," she replied. I was agitated by then in our conversation and said to her, "When you show up late you are stealing from the company, you are angering your peers who have to pick up your slack, and consequently your misbehavior is annoying me. If you do not modify your routine and show up on time—we will take this to the next disciplinary level. Understood?" She nodded in agreement and left my office. I wish I could report to you our brief chat fixed the problem, but it did not. She no longer works for the organization.

Telling people the truth about their behavior and how it impacts you doesn't always turn out perfectly. Remember, the responsibility for the way a person responds to you is up to them. Your responsibility is to speak the truth in love.

When I was a lead pastor, I did not fully understand this principle. I was uneven with how I applied it. I did well speaking the truth in love to most of the people in the congregation. I struggled with stronger personalities, especially those who were key leaders. When they crossed a boundary, I tended to stuff my feelings out of fear rather than deal with the issue directly. This inconsistency was a key contributor to my battle with depression.

If you want to get healthy emotionally and stay that way, you have to make Choice 2 part of your life—you have to manage your anger. The good news is you are capable. You can learn how to talk with people just like I did to the sales executive and to my direct report. You can discover how to express strong feelings in a way that honors God and keeps you emotionally healthy at the same time. If you choose to cling to unhealthy patterns of dealing with anger, rage will ruin your life—or someone else's.

Responding to your anger with aggression hurts others. Responding to it passively hurts yourself. Expressing it assertively and in love, helps build a strong emotional foundation for your life, and provides a good model for others to follow.

But your work is not finished. Another choice is required. You must learn how to protect yourself from abuse.

Before starting the next chapter, take a minute to say the following *I-CHOOSE* statement:

I CHOOSE TO MANAGE MY ANGER INSTEAD OF IT MANAGING ME

CHOICE 3
PROTECT YOURSELF FROM ABUSE

Abusive people are proliferating in our increasingly dysfunctional world. An abusive or toxic personality is defined simply as one who harms people either verbally, emotionally, physically, sexually, or spiritually. These types of people refuse to allow you to hold an opinion contrary to their own. They seek to manipulate you through coercion, false guilt, and fear. Their primary interest is not to relate with you—it is to control you. Developing the ability to spot them before they hurt you will save you a significant amount of grief. We need a finely tuned *jerkometer*, (the ability to spot jerks), to protect ourselves.

Many years ago, I made a huge hiring mistake. Trying to fill a critical role on my team, I felt a sense of urgency to close the loop. I had interviewed four candidates with no progress and was getting a bit panicky. In front of me was the fifth candidate—a person with an impressive resumé, who displayed great charisma and confidence throughout the interview. By all outward measurements, hiring him was a no-brainer. During the entire interview however, I had serious internal misgivings about this person. Call it intuition, discernment, whatever, I blew by those intuitive warning flags and hired the guy. Big mistake. He nearly destroyed my team, and I ended up firing him. How could I miss so badly on this hire? One reason was I ignored my internal jerkometer—and paid a heavy price.

Protecting yourself from abusive people is the third choice of emotionally healthy people. This choice includes establishing and enforcing healthy relational boundaries. It requires you to understand the special relational dynamics introduced by a malicious personality.

A perfect example of toxic personalities can be found in the Gospel of John, chapter nine. Here we see an abusive response by the Pharisees to a man born blind. He was miraculously healed by Jesus. When he gave credit to Christ for his miracle, the Pharisees reacted by using fear and intimidation in an attempt to get this guy to change his story. When the healed man stood his ground, the religious leaders brought out the big guns, and threw him out of the synagogue.

Emotionally healthy people avoid putting themselves in the path of abusive people. And when they cannot detour around them, they do not allow jerky people to damage their emotional well-being.

In 2 Timothy 4:14-15, the apostle Paul provided clear direction on this subject to the young pastor, Timothy. *"Alexander the metalworker did me a great deal of harm. The Lord will repay him for what he has done. You too should be on your guard against him, because he strongly opposed our message."* The phrase, *"Be on your guard,"* comes from the Greek word *"pulasso."* The way it is used here suggests *"to keep away from."*

I probably do not need to tell you this, but at some level, abusive personalities live in your neighborhood, or they work at your company—or unfortunately—may be part of your family. Apparently Alexander the metalworker was an abuser. His tendency toward relationally destructive behavior made him dangerous. Whenever it is possible and practical, Paul taught us here to avoid these types of people. When it is not possible or practical, here are some safeguards you can use to protect yourself:

1. Stand up for yourself

Standing up for yourself is the cornerstone of protecting yourself from toxic people. You must become convinced this is the right thing to do. If you don't, you are going to struggle with controlling personalities. It helps when you realize even Jesus didn't allow anyone to push Him around until His hour had come.

When one of my sons was in third grade, he was getting knocked around every day during recess by a much larger schoolmate. My son was understandably upset by this ongoing behavior, so I sketched out a strategy for him to deal with it. "The next time Guber (not his schoolmate's real name) puts his hands on you, I want you to ball up your fist and swing as hard as you can and pop him in the nose." The very next day the drama unfolded. Guber started shoving my son around again and he responded with a right cross to Guber's schnazz. Problem solved. Yes, I realize this was not politically correct, and I had to smooth things over with the principal, but Guber never bullied my son again.

I'm not recommending you start punching out people in your neighborhood, workplace, or family. The point here is when you are confronted with abuse from a toxic personality, understand you have the right to draw a clear relational boundary and protect yourself from his poor behavior.

Suppose a family member verbally takes advantage of you. You have been direct with him about how his misbehavior affects you, but he continues to treat you poorly with his words. A healthy relational boundary simply informs your abuser what you will (or will not) do in response to his actions. "If you keep insulting me, I'll go to another room in the house."

After teaching on this subject one evening, a person who was in his thirties said: "Every time I go over to my mother's house, she criticizes me and berates me. What should I do?" My response was: "Why do you still go over there every week? Set a boundary: 'Mom, here is how your verbal abuse affects me. I feel belittled, hurt, and angry. If you continue, I won't visit you anymore.'" Boundaries aren't a crowbar to get people who hurt you to change their behavior. They simply protect you from their behavior. If their actions change, it's a bonus. Proverbs 11:9 states, *"With his mouth the godless destroys his neighbor, but through knowledge the righteous escape."* The first safeguard? Stand up for yourself.

2. Understand the difference between persecution and abuse

Being persecuted for your faith is different than being abused by someone who is simply obnoxious. In Matthew 5:11, Jesus told His disciples, *"Blessed are you when people insult you, persecute you and falsely say all kinds of evil against you **because of Me**"* [emphasis added]. My son wasn't being persecuted on the playground, he was being bullied.

Getting persecuted because we refuse to compromise our morals, or let go of our integrity, or deny Jesus, is different than getting knocked around by a bully on a playground. Protecting ourselves requires us to distinguish between mistreatment related to our faith versus simply being in the path of a mean-spirited person. Don't confuse the two scenarios—they are not the same.

3. Identify your own unhealthy relational patterns

This can be a painful exercise, but examining your family of origin can pay off. Think about your family background for a minute. How did your family relate to each other? How did you handle anger, conflict, or disappointment? If your family was toxic, you have a higher probability of subconsciously being drawn to abusive people. The familiar often draws us—even if it is unhealthy. It can be less intimidating than a healthy environment which is *unfamiliar* to you. Messed up, isn't it?

In fact, being around healthy people may seem boring to you if you grew up in an emotionally destructive home. A pastor friend relayed the following story to me: A husband who had been out of work for years finally landed a good job. Within two months, his wife asked for a divorce. My friend was stunned. He had spent numerous hours "pre-job" encouraging the couple to hang in there. Why would the wife ask for a divorce right on the heels of their prayers being answered? As he dug deeper, he learned the environment the wife grew up in was chaotic—she had lived with an alcoholic father. His addiction produced considerable drama in the home which spilled over into his work life. She had become accustomed to dysfunction—in a sick way, it was comfortable to her. And when the chaos in her marriage was reduced, apparently she could not handle a healthier normal.

4. Spend time with healthy people

You need to be deliberate about this objective. Finding a circle of good friends will provide a measure of protection from abusive relationships. It will give you the support you need to break free from your abuser.

SPEND TIME WITH HEALTHY PEOPLE

Understand healthy people are not perfect—we are all works-in-progress. A good friend gives you permission to be human, does not try to control you, is trustworthy, and allows you to express your opinion—even when it is contrary to hers.

Choose wisely who you spend your discretionary time with and your emotional health will prosper. Proverbs 13:20 teaches us: *"He who walks with the wise grows wise, but a companion of fools suffers harm."*

ABUSERS HAVE A WARPED VERSION OF REALITY

5. Practice loving yourself when attacked

When abusive people try to intimidate or victimize you, keep telling yourself the truth: "I am loved and respected by God. I am a capable person. I don't deserve to be treated this way." When we respond like this we create a safe zone around our emotions. It helps us to understand the behavior is their issue, not ours.

In 1 Kings 18 we see King Ahab holding a conference with the prophet Elijah. In verse 17 his initial greeting to Elijah was: *"Is that you, you troubler of Israel?"* Ironic isn't it? Ahab was described in 1 Kings as a leader who *"did more evil in the eyes of the Lord than any of those before him."* His wife Jezebel was even worse. It was their evil, idolatrous, and abusive behavior that brought trouble upon Israel. Yet here we see Ahab blaming the prophet for the mess the king and his wife themselves created.

Ahab's warped version of reality is characteristic of abusive personalities. No matter how distorted and inaccurate their version of an event is, they absolutely believe their account is the truth. Protect yourself from people who operate at this level of self-deception by practicing healthy self-talk when they attack you.

6. Understand what "loving your enemy" really means

It is not loving to let someone abuse you. In Matt. 5:43-44 Jesus taught His disciples: *"You have heard that it was said, 'love your neighbor, but hate your enemy.' But I tell you: Love your enemies."*

He was addressing the Old Testament Scripture in Leviticus 19: *"Love your neighbor as yourself."* Somewhere along the line *"hate your enemy"* was added to the end of the verse— probably by the teachers of the Law. Jesus took issue with the idea by declaring: Love your neighbor—but love your enemy too.

IT'S NOT LOVING TO LET SOMEONE ABUSE YOU

Confusion comes when we misinterpret Jesus' intent here. What was He trying to tell us? Two things stand out to me. First, Jesus was teaching us not to allow hatred to find a place in our heart because it's cancerous—and left unchecked, it will destroy us. Hatred usually damages the hater more than the target of their hate.

The second thing standing out in Matthew 5:43-44 comes in the form of a question: What does it mean to genuinely love our enemies? If someone is verbally abusing you, he is *sinning*. Does real love just sit there and take it? Or does real love hold him accountable for his behavior? Is it

YOU ARE RESPONSIBLE TO PROTECT YOURSELF

not true this type of sinning is hurting him too? Is it more loving to let him continue harming himself while he's hurting you—or to draw a line in the sand with the dual intention of protecting yourself and seeing him repent? You are not responsible for his repentance—but you are responsible to protect yourself.

Loving your enemy means you care about them and want God's best for them. It can even include praying for them. However, love does not mean you allow them to take advantage of you.

7. Consistently address abuse when it happens

Let me tell you the story of Lou Ann (not her real name). I was teaching in her church a while back, and after speaking on the subject of protecting oneself from abuse, she came up to chat. Lou Ann was in her mid-to-late 40s and lived with a verbally abusive dad. He was a recent widower, and once his wife was gone, she became his new verbal punching bag. She told me: "If I just put up with it a while longer, maybe he'll come to the Lord." I asked her: "Has he gotten noticeably closer to following Christ in the last year?" Her response was: "Well, no." Then I asked her: "And how are *you* feeling?" She responded: "I'm exhausted. I'm running on fumes."

How can that scenario be right? Both parties in the relationship are losing. Lou Ann would have been much better off to tell her dad: "I love you, dad, but your verbal insults hurt me deeply. If you continue to treat me this way, I will leave the room." If he didn't get the message, moving out might be the next step in setting a proper boundary with her father. Instead, she absorbed his cruelty and ended up emotionally fragile and exhausted.

The reality is if we do not tell the truth to the abusive people in our lives, if we tolerate their actions without standing up for ourselves, deep down we end up resenting them anyway. And I don't know about you, but I have a hard time even wanting to be near someone I resent, much less trying to win them to Christ.

A better way is available—tell the offender how his behavior is negatively impacting you. Speak the truth in love. And let him know what you will do to protect yourself when he acts poorly. Chances are he will not understand your response right away and may even react to you harshly. Stay consistent and over time he should get the message. If he does not, avoid this person whenever possible.

Now let me say something which may be difficult to accept. If the abuse has become physical in nature—you must understand a line has been crossed. You need to put some geographic distance between you and your abuser. Find a shelter—get a restraining order if necessary. Surround yourself with supportive, loving people. Distance offers some protection to you, and gives your abuser time to work on his or her issues.

It deeply troubles me when I read 60% of girls in dating relationships report some form of physical abuse. Young ladies— there is never a legitimate reason for the young man you are dating to put his hands on you in anger, or in any other way which makes you uncomfortable. If he misbehaves this way, say goodbye to him and move on with your life—he doesn't deserve you.

Choice 3 is critical to developing and maintaining emotional health. Pay attention to your jerkometer. If you are serious about being emotionally fit, you must learn to protect yourself from difficult and dangerous people. And the good news is with practice, you can develop this skill—and reduce your risk of relational injury.

In the next chapter, we'll consider perhaps the most neglected choice preventing us from enjoying emotional well-being: refueling emotionally.

Before you proceed, take a moment to say out loud the following *I-CHOOSE* statement:

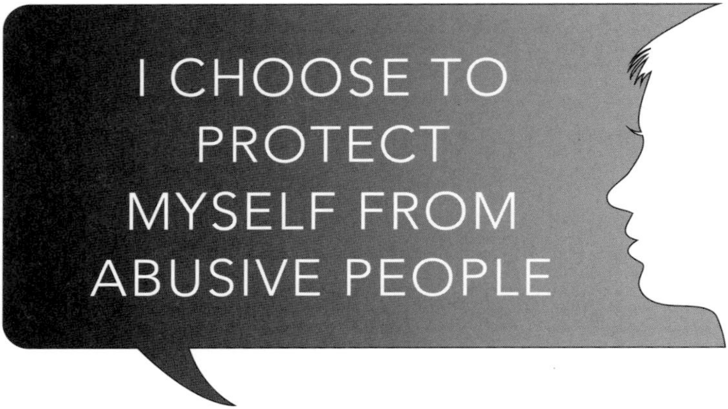
I CHOOSE TO
PROTECT
MYSELF FROM
ABUSIVE PEOPLE

CHOICE 4
REFUEL EMOTIONALLY

Several years ago I drove an awesome red truck. The day I brought it home from the dealership, my wife's first response was: "Oh, that's a cute truck!"—Not exactly the response I was looking for. Manly—yes. Awesome—certainly. Cute? Never!

The truck had an RPM gauge with a red line. I noticed the only time the RPM needle came close to the red boundary was when I punched the accelerator to pass other vehicles. Even when cruising at 70 mph, the gauge indicator never came close to the red RPM border. To operate my truck near the red line for extended periods of time would have been irresponsible.

Funny, we know better than to treat our vehicle's engine poorly, yet we don't always know better when it comes to our emotional engine. We often run at peak emotional RPMs for extended periods without giving ourselves time to wind down. Or, we consistently operate on emotional

> WE NEED TIME TO COOL OFF AND REFUEL

fumes. God never intended for us to live this way. We need time to cool off and refuel.

Refueling emotionally is the fourth choice of emotionally healthy people. It has nothing to do with being ruled by our feelings. It has everything to do with *paying attention* to them.

This choice is the great frontier for many of us. The idea of a balanced cadence of work and rest flies in the face of modern culture.

The 1980s gave us a new corporate work ethic summarized by two phrases: "churn 'em and burn 'em." Large software companies would hire programmers upon their graduation from college and work them 70 hours per week until they burned out. Then those companies would fire them and hire a new group of graduates.

Unfortunately, the 21st century hasn't brought much relief in terms of work-week length. A 2014 Gallup poll discovered 40% of U.S. full-time workers are working between 50-70 hours per week. What are we doing to ourselves? We live in a culture where more people are becoming addicted to adrenaline—and are enslaved by an unsustainable pace. As a result, we are running on empty emotionally. We need to refuel.

When I ask people if they have ever been taught how to do this, the answer is always "No." Yet the Bible is full of references to this principle. Jesus invites us: *"Come to me, all you who are weary and burdened, and I will give you rest. Take my yoke upon you and learn from me, for I am gentle and humble in heart, and you will find rest for your souls. For my yoke is easy and my burden is light"* (Matthew 11:28-30). The goal of this chapter is to learn how to incorporate Jesus' invitation into our personal life.

When it comes to emotional fuel, three baselines are critical:

1. You can't give what you don't have

If you have no money in your wallet, or no money in your back account, how much money can you give to those in need? Zero. If you have little-to-no fuel in your emotional tank, it is difficult to demonstrate compassion for people—not because you are a bad person—but because you have nothing left to give.

2. You are an emotional being

We consist of more than just body and spirit. We are three-part beings: body, spirit, and soul. And the soul component includes our emotions. I am puzzled by well-meaning Christians who say: "If I pay attention to the spiritual part of my life, the rest will be taken care of. Why would I need to focus any time or energy on my feelings?" To which I respond: "So if you take care of your spiritual life, there is no need to pay attention to your body? You can eat whatever you want and be a couch potato with no negative effects on your health?" Their line of thinking is faulty. A well-rounded person pays attention to all three elements: body, spirit, *and* soul.

3. You have to pay attention to your emotions

Three key indicators give you clues regarding the level of emotional fuel you have in your tank:

a. Your pace

Your importance to God has very little to do with how full your schedule looks. Pace does not equal value. So, let me ask you, are you maintaining a reasonable stride? When I was a youth pastor at a large church my schedule was routinely packed. One day I remember calling my best friend, who was a lead pastor at another church, and bragging I had 28 out of 30 nights scheduled in a particular month. I was waiting for him to commend me on what a dedicated servant of God I was, when he shot back two simple words: "Stop sinning!" I was stunned. After an awkward silence,

PACE DOES NOT EQUAL VALUE

he continued: "You are sinning against your family and against yourself. Knock it off!" Not the response I was looking for, but he was spot-on. Not only was I sinning against my family and myself, I was *lying* to myself by believing I could sustain such a crazy pace and not eventually pay a price.

I hate to tell you this (not really)—but multiple studies reveal once you reach eight hours of work in any given day, your best production is behind you. Henry Ford figured this out in the early 1900s. He reduced the workday of his factory employees to eight hours, and saw their productivity and Ford's bottom line soar.

Beyond eight hours in a day, we create only a small fraction of our normal output. The problem is many of us work ten-to-twelve-hour days *every day*. And we fool ourselves into thinking longer hours equal more output.

If you lean toward workaholic tendencies, I'm not suggesting you overreact by swinging to the opposite extreme of laziness. Slothfulness isn't the answer. Neither is avoiding the use of your gifts to serve God and others. Sensible scheduling is a healthier response.

In his classic book, *The Power of Positive Thinking*, Dr. Norman Vincent Peale wrote: "It is impossible to have peace of soul if the pace is so feverishly accelerated. *God won't go that fast* [emphasis added]. He will not endeavor to keep up with you. He says in effect, 'Go ahead if you must with this foolish pace and when you are worn out I will offer My healing . . .' The only wise rate at which to live is God's rate. God gets things done and they are done right and He does them without hurry."[1]

If you want to be emotionally fit, you need to refuel at regular intervals. And refueling requires you to pay attention to your pace. One of the more deceptive traps of life is running too fast because of all the important things we have to do. Christians tend to rationalize hectic calendars by telling themselves they are doing it for the kingdom of God.

In the book of Genesis we see God created the entire universe in six days and rested on the seventh. He didn't rest because He was tired. He did it to set an example. We make a mistake when we set a work pace even God didn't choose for Himself. Establishing a reasonable work-rest rhythm makes you a more effective and productive spouse, parent, worker, or student. Paying attention to pace includes:

i. Learning to live out of rest

Wayne Cordeiro states: "When we rest, God continues His work."[2] Consider his brief yet profound statement for a moment and let it sink in. "When we rest, God continues His work." We tend to believe when we take a breather, God's work stops—or when we sleep—God nods off too. We think nothing gets done unless we personally lead the charge. The result of believing this lie can cause us to overcommit and overschedule. The result often is burn-out or depression—and in the long run—less productivity.

The Bible promotes the principle of living out of rest in both the Old and New Testaments. We have already referred to Jesus' call to slow down in Matthew 11. He understood how to live this way. When you observe Him in the Gospels, you discover He was never stressed out, except in the Garden of Gethsemane (understandably). Jesus never appeared to be in a hurry.

He was purposeful without being harried. He resisted the temptation to allow other people's expectations to influence His priorities.

A prime example is when Jesus learned His good friend Lazarus was seriously ill. Instead of dropping everything and heading for Bethany, He stayed put for two days. Even when Jesus became aware Lazarus had died, He told His disciples in John 11, *"Let us go back to Judea."* And by the time He finally got to Bethany, His friend had been dead four days. Jesus was not being uncaring or irresponsible in this circumstance. He was demonstrating that He operated on His Father's timetable and nobody else's. He modeled an emotionally healthy choice. He wasn't encouraging us to skip a friend's funeral. Rather, He was teaching us to refuse to allow other people to set our priorities.

In John 5:19, He announced: *"I tell you the truth, the Son can do nothing by himself; He can only do what He sees His Father doing, because whatever the Father does the Son also does."* Jesus only did what He saw His Father doing. Nothing more—nothing less. And yet, He was incredibly productive.

If Jesus is our model, why are we Christians so stressed out? Could it be possible we have taken on some responsibilities God never intended? Jesus practiced the principle of living and working out of rest. He invites us to assume His yoke and burden, instead of our own. He wants us to follow His agenda and priorities instead of ours, or those others would like to place on us.

Let's look at an Old Testament figure who understood the concept of living out of rest. David is considered by many to be the greatest king in the Old Testament. In Acts 13:22 we see God identified him as a *"man after My own heart."* He certainly was not a perfect man. David made several huge mistakes, but Israel enjoyed some of its greatest years when he was their leader.

David was the poster child for action and achievement. Psalm 23, his most well-known writing, reveals several secrets to his success. *"He (God) makes me lie down in green pastures. He leads me beside quiet waters. He restores my soul. He guides me in paths of righteousness . . . my cup overflows"* (Psalm 23:2-3a; 5c).

Here we discover David's simple recipe for living well:

> • Follow God as He leads you into "green pastures" and by "quiet waters." As He brings you to places of solitude, linger there.
> • Allow Him to rejuvenate you in those places. This helps you live out of the overflow produced in those quiet, reflective moments.
> • Let Him clarify precisely what He is requiring you to do, and what He is not asking you to do. Wayne Cordeiro states: "We won't be held accountable for how much we have done, but for how much we have done of what He has asked us to do."[3]

Paying attention to pace means you learn how to live from a foundation of rest. Yet other components of this indicator exist which you need to monitor.

ii. Take a day off weekly

A day off means more than simply not showing up at work. It includes resisting the urge to read work-related

THE DISTANCE BETWEEN WORKAHOLISM AND ARROGANCE IS SHORT

emails on your day off. It involves putting the smartphone on silent and keeping it as far away from you as possible. If you have an emergency that swallows up your day off, then try to compensate the following week by taking additional time off. Avoid the practice of allowing multiple weeks to run together with no down-time.

God gave us the Sabbath as a weekly reset button—a day to downshift, relax, and rest. Pushing this weekly reset button recalibrates our:

- **Perspective**

A day off reminds us our life's work is ultimately God's, not ours. The distance between workaholism and arrogance is short. When we regularly disregard God's command to rest, it's easy to take all the credit for our success. The apostle Paul had a different view: *"I planted the seed, Apollos watered it, but God made it grow."* (1 Corinthians 3:6).

- **Permanence**

The reset button extends our shelf-life. Rest at proper intervals actually increases our productivity. God can get more done through us over a longer period of time when we take a regular day off.

- **Priorities**

The weekly day of rest gets us back in touch with what truly matters. It reminds us our spouse and children are more important than our careers or material possessions. It gets us back in touch with life outside of work.

iii. Learn when to stop

Watching the pace indicator means listening to your body and your brain. After a certain number of hours in a day or week, you get tired. Welcome to humanity. When you are genuinely tired, accept it as a God-given stop-signal instead of blowing by it and pushing through. Avoid the faulty logic after a full day of work: "If I just put in three more hours, I'll get ahead." This kind of approach is like digging in sand. Ever tried to dig a hole in sand? The crater just keeps getting filled in with more gravel collapsing in from the sides. Even when you work the additional three hours, have you noticed your schedule mysteriously gets filled up with more things to do?

A while ago I read an excellent article written by Tony Schwartz, titled, *"The Magic of Doing One Thing at a Time."* One of the best sections in the article states: "It's not just the number of hours we're working, but also the fact that we spend too many continuous hours juggling too many things at the same time. What we've lost, above all, are stopping points, finish lines, and boundaries."[4]

iv. Develop the habit of weekly solitude

Finding a place to get alone weekly can help normalize our pace. Every Saturday morning I spend 15-20 minutes in total quietness by myself. I get up early to avoid noise and outside interference. I open my journal in anticipation that God will drop inspired thoughts into my mind and heart.

The focus of this quiet time includes thinking about how good God is—meditating on what He has done for me and those I care about. This Saturday retreat is usually the most productive prayer time of my entire week. I don't talk to Him—rather I just sit quietly and listen. I encourage you to try this out. See if solitude helps you to regulate your pace and refuel your tank.

v. Commit to rest even during busy seasons

The pace indicator requires special attention when we're knee-deep in work. When I was young, my dad told me: "John, you have to make hay while the sun shines." He meant I needed to work whenever the opportunity presented itself, because I might miss out if I didn't. This thought process drove dad to work two jobs for a large portion of his life. I am certain having to feed and clothe nine children motivated him as well. I appreciate the work-ethic my dad imparted to me, but there are some problems with this philosophical approach.

In our western culture, it is tempting to live by the "make hay while the sun shines" mantra. Good things are happening, your business or sports career is ascending, and opportunity waits around every corner. The temptation to "make hay while the sun shines" can be difficult to resist. We try to ride the wave for as long as we can, often ignoring our need for rest.

In Exodus 31:13a God commanded Moses: *"Say to the Israelites, 'You must observe my Sabbaths.'"* And in Exodus 34:21: *"Six days you shall labor, but on the seventh day you shall rest; even during the plowing season* *and harvest you **must** rest"* [emphasis added].

We see the principle of Sabbath-rest extend to the New Testament: *"There remains, then, a Sabbath-rest for the people of God; for anyone who enters God's rest also rests from his own work, just as God did from his. Let us, therefore, make every effort to enter that rest, so that no one will fall by following their example of disobedience"* (Hebrews 4:9-11).

Regular rest is more than a good idea—it is a mandate from God. He commanded the Israelites to observe the Sabbath even during times of "plowing and harvest." For a farmer, these represent the busiest times of the year.

> REGULAR REST IS A MANDATE FROM GOD

Yet, even in those seasons, God made it clear rest was not optional—it was essential. When a busy stretch appears on the horizon, deliberately make room in your schedule for rest, relaxation, and renewal. Block off time in your calendar for these pursuits and guard them carefully. This may cut across the grain of the way you think, but if you lose your health, you greatly diminish your ability to produce.

A friend once told me: "I'll rest when I die." To which I replied: "You are going to get there faster than God wants you to." I added: "How does your wife feel about that?" Another friend said to me: "Sleep is a disposable commodity." My response was: "Research doesn't back up your statement and neither does God's word: *"In vain you rise early and stay up late, toiling for food to eat— for He grants sleep to those he loves"* (Psalm 127:2).

Another friend told me: "I'll slow down after five years when I get my company up, running, and solidified." To which I replied: "So let me get this straight, you are going to disobey God for the next five years, and you're OK with it? And you think He's OK with it?"

Changing a workaholic pattern is not like flipping an on/off switch. It is difficult to unlearn dysfunctional patterns of working and replace them with healthy ones. Cordeiro writes: "We have learned to rest when the work is done. But the fact of the matter is the work will never be done. There will always be more to do. So Sabbath-rest becomes a command to respond to, not a result of nothing left to do."[5]

It's time to stop the schedule insanity—to decide we won't allow the frantic pace of our culture to squeeze us into its mold. The rat race seduces us. Success . . . recognition . . . wealth. But it usually promises more than it actually delivers.

vi. Prioritize

Watching the pace indicator is easier when you write down your priorities, and concentrate on the top seven for the next 90 days. Focus is powerful. It increases our productivity and forces us to ignore less strategic tasks. It reminds us there will always be more work to do than time to do it. Focus contributes to a healthy pace.

I repeat this prioritization activity at the beginning of every quarter. I review my ten-year, three-year, and one-year targets, and reprioritize my 90-day goals accordingly.

vii. Match your output with your input

Paying attention to pace means figuring out what activities drain you and which ones replenish you—and then balancing your schedule accordingly. If your calendar is full of draining tasks, and light on replenishing ones, become more intentional about adding refreshing ones to your calendar.

viii. Understand the law of diminishing returns

Pace monitoring means being honest with ourselves. When we overwork on a regular basis it gets increasingly harder for us to recover emotionally. I lift weights three-to-four times per week. I need days off in-between to let the stretched muscles recover. Lifting weights every day actually inhibits fitness. I would experience the law of diminishing returns.

Once we reach 40 hours in a work week, our productivity quickly heads south. The law of diminishing returns applies to everyone, whether you are a pastor, farmer, doctor, teacher, or businessperson. It is simply part of being human. And if we regularly put in 55-60 hours a week—or more—we are tearing emotional muscles without giving them sufficient time to heal. Our unbalanced approach catapults us toward burnout. And when we reach the burnout stage, our output is severely diminished.

ix. Separate work from your personal life

Separation is the last item we'll consider on the pace gauge. Shutting off work is easy to write about, but much harder to practice. The line between work and our personal life is blurrier than ever. I used to answer emails after hours, on weekends, and even on vacations. Many of my colleagues still do—but I am refusing to re-join that group. I'm doing this not out of laziness, but out of principle. If my company needs me to be available 24/7, then something is wrong with me, or my company, or both.

Disconnecting from work means shutting off your computer when you get home. Turn off the sound indicators on your smartphone signaling an email or text message. If you don't, you will be tempted to look and all of a sudden the separation you are attempting to gain is lost. It only takes one email or text message to get the work wheels spinning.

Pace is one of the most important indicators on your emotional gauge. The apostles learned this firsthand from Jesus: *"The apostles gathered around Jesus and reported to him all they had done and taught. Then, because so many people were coming and going that they did not even have a chance to eat, he said to them, 'Come with me by yourselves to a quiet place and get some rest.' So they went away by themselves in a boat to a solitary place"* (Mark 6:30-32).

Disconnecting from work is not wasted time or selfish behavior. Rather, it is a crucial part of maintaining balance in the face of the ever-present demands of our culture.

The second emotional indicator requiring attention is:

b. Your personal relationships

As we noted earlier, the line between your career and your personal life can be fuzzy. The day-to-day firefighting of work, or maintaining your house, etc., can leave you worn out and often feeling too tired for the important work of friendship building.

When was the last time you hung out with your companions just to have fun? Ecclesiastes 4:9 points out *"Two are better than one, because they have a good return for their work."*

We get a better emotional return in life when we're linked up with other like-minded individuals. Prolonged isolation leads to trouble. Make friends a part of your weekly schedule. And if you are struggling to find quality friends, here are several ideas which may help:

i. Join an organization aligning with your interests or hobbies. Golf and bowling leagues are everywhere. If you like to build things with your hands, join Habitat for Humanity or a similar organization.

ii. Use technology to your advantage. Skype or Face-Time are excellent ways to stay in touch with long-distance friends.

iii. Smile when you meet people. I need to work on this one. A genuine smile is both magnetic and disarming. If you walk with the weight of the world on your face, people will tend to avoid you.

iv. Become a good listener. Someone told me a long time ago: "The subject of highest interest to most people is themselves." Learn how to ask questions that allow others to talk to you about what's going on in their lives. Avoid the temptation to focus on yourself.

The third emotional indicator you need to monitor is:

c. Your plan

My car has a maintenance plan. I change the oil every several thousand miles and rotate the tires. The purpose is to extend the vehicle's life. Just like I have a strategy to maintain my car, you can make choices to help maintain your emotions. Below are some emotional maintenance items. None of these will be earth-shattering or new revelations. This is stuff you probably have heard before. What you know is important—but it's what you do with what you know that makes a real difference. The following choices are not quick fixes; they need to become your lifestyle. The refueling process is not like jump-starting a dead battery. The negative effects of running your life for years on the edge schedule-wise will not be reversed in a week.

Emotional maintenance items include:

i. Laughter

Proverbs 17:22 states: *"A cheerful heart is good medicine, but a crushed spirit dries up the bones."* Laughter is a strategic part of emotional maintenance. Ever felt better after a good belly laugh? The feel-good rush we experience is chemical in nature. Scientific research confirms chuckling releases endorphins which reduce stress hormone levels and elevate our mood. Regular doses of good clean fun replenish our emotional reserves.

Earlier in this book I detailed my battle with clinical depression. One of the key strategies I applied while recovering was what I like to call comedy therapy. In the depths of my emotional darkness, watching my favorite funny movie on a regular basis made me laugh and helped me heal.

Life can squeeze the joy out of you. If you want to maintain proper emotional fuel levels you need to add some wholesome fun to your schedule.

ii. Exercise

Much like laughter, exercise is a key part of an emotional maintenance plan. It helps us burn off nervous energy and lower our stress levels. Some researchers disagree with the idea of a positive relationship between working out and emotional well-being. But for me personally, when I've had a stressful day, there is nothing like pounding the weights at the gym to bring relief. Walking outside is effective too. At the onset of my depression, I did not belong to a gym and we didn't have a weight set at home—so I walked every day, regardless of the weather. I found my mood improved when I did this.

Some Jesus-followers point at Paul's words to the young pastor Timothy in 1 Timothy 4:8 as their rationale for avoiding exercise: *"For physical training is of some value, but godliness has value for all things . . ."* Notice Paul did not say here physical training was of no value. He said it was of some value.

Many research scientists suggest exercise can be as effective as antidepressant medication in elevating our mood. I am not suggesting you need to become a bodybuilder or a marathon runner to maintain good emotional health. But you do need to get your body moving. Exercise is a good use of your time and helps most people refuel emotionally. Check with your doctor before beginning any workout program.

Let me digress here momentarily to touch on the subject of medication. A general bias exists in the Church against using antidepressants. When it surfaces at Q&A sessions I ask: "How many of you take pain reliever for a headache? How many of you would have no problem taking insulin if you were diabetic? Would you use pain medication if you were recovering from surgery?" "How about taking an antibiotic when you have an infection?"

Taking advantage of antidepressant medication when you are depressed is no different. It has the potential to stabilize you so you are able to work on the roots of the affliction. Be aware medication alone will not bring full recovery—but it allows a better chance for healing to occur. Work closely and collaboratively with your doctor when it comes to using medication.

iii. Boredom

Some of you need to inject a little "boring" in your plan. God did not wire you to be on high alert 24/7. Remember, you are made in His image, and He rested from the work of creation on the seventh day.

Plant some flowers; play 18-holes; visit a museum; take a walk on the beach. For our 25th wedding anniversary I surprised my wife with ballroom dancing lessons. When you are learning how to do the rumba, you have no time to think about anything serious. And when you're not thinking about anything serious for an hour—it can be refreshing. If you want to refuel emotionally, you'll have a better chance of success if you learn how to inject a bit of boring into your life.

iv. Emotional tenacity

Emotional tenacity is a key contributor to emotional upkeep. It combines the qualities of love, kindness, truth, and strength. Emotional toughness requires us to become comfortable speaking the truth in love. It's a critical skill for us to develop if we want to keep our emotional tank full.

We see this behavior operating in the lives of Moses and Jesus. According to the Bible, Moses was the meekest man on earth during his lifetime. Yet we notice him experiencing the emotion of righteous anger when the Israelites worshipped the golden calf. Jesus was sinless, yet we see Him feel and express strong emotion on multiple occasions, usually when He saw people being ripped off under the guise of religion. In one instance, He overturned the money-changers' tables in the temple and drove them out with a whip.

We are not Moses or Jesus. So what does emotional tenacity look like for us? At a high-level, it means understanding there is a time to be legitimately angry. Some situations require us to be strong and firm. Strength and firmness can and should coexist with love. Emotional toughness enhances our health. Failure to develop it sets us up to get pushed around—and getting pushed around makes it harder to maintain proper fuel levels.

Obviously, refueling emotionally takes practice—especially for Type-A personalities. It requires us to think and act counter-culturally. We live in a nation where being part of the rat race is expected, saluted, honored, and cheered. What once was thought of as a ridiculous pace has become the new normal.

The old expression, "I'd rather burn out for God than rust out" sounds heroic, but in reality is a short-sighted and dangerous mentality. If adopted, it reduces our shelf-life.

The problem is, many of us are proud of our busy-ness. For some, it has become our identity. The question is, why? Why do we work this way? A number of reasons exist, but at the root, *we are afraid.*

We may be afraid of not having enough money. The uncertainty of our economy, plus the current lack of corporate loyalty to employees puts us on edge financially. Others of us are fearful of public opinion. We can care way too much what other people think about us, and let their expectations set our calendar. Some of us are worried about losing relationships. We're concerned if we fail to measure up to the unrealistic expectations of family, friends, and work peers, they'll shut us out. These worries are understandable—but a fear-based approach to life and work is a recipe for anxiety, burnout, and depression.

Remember Psalm 23:1-3a: *"The Lord is my shepherd, I shall not be in want. He makes me lie down in green pastures, he leads me beside quiet waters, He restores my soul."* To be emotionally healthy, learn how and when to take your foot off the gas pedal so you can rest, recharge, and refuel.

In the following chapter we will consider the fifth choice of emotionally healthy people. Before you proceed, take a minute to say the following *I-CHOOSE* statement:

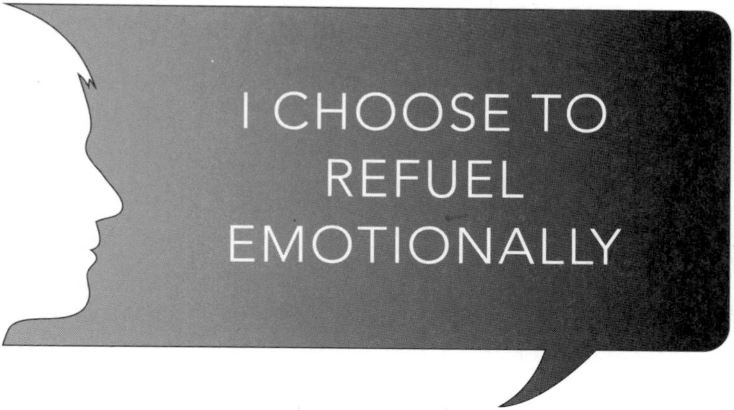
I CHOOSE TO
REFUEL
EMOTIONALLY

CHOICE 5
STAY ALERT

The fifth choice of emotionally healthy people is to stay alert. Traps lurk and threaten your emotional well-being. Staying alert means being aware of those pitfalls and remaining sensitive to the warning signs indicating you may be flirting with depression.

If you have come through the long dark tunnel of depression and are enjoying life again—beware. Once you stabilize emotionally, and begin to work on identifying the roots of your depression, eventually you will begin to feel better. Emotional normalcy will gradually return to you. But be advised—this is the point where several traps lurk which can bring your recovery to a grinding halt.

1. Depression becomes your identity long-term

The trap of depression becoming your long-term identity is usually sprung after you are well on your way to getting better. In the short term, it is your identity to a large degree, because depression has the ability to envelop you. Recovery can take a long time even when taking the necessary steps to heal. But continuing to see yourself as a victim will hinder your healing process. *"For God did not give us a spirit of timidity, but a spirit of power, of love and of self-discipline"* (2 Timothy 1:7). This is your long-term identity if you belong to Christ.

I believe depression is a whole-person problem and consequently it needs to be addressed on multiple fronts simultaneously. It possesses many components: physical, emotional, spiritual, and your schedule. Getting better requires a full-court press—attack your opponent on several fronts:

a. Take care of your body

Regular exercise and healthy eating contribute to better mental and physical fitness. Work with experts in these fields to pull together an effective strategy.

b. Fill your emotional tank

Replenishing relationships and enjoyable recreational activities can energize you. Block off time in your calendar for friends and fun.

c. Reject the devil's lies

The vast majority of depression is not demonic in nature—but it's easier for Satan to whisper lies when you're depressed. You may need the help of wise, trusted friends to identify his fibs.

d. Take control of your schedule

Being sensible with your calendar brings stability. Finding a healthy work/rest rhythm takes practice.

This no-holds-barred approach prevents depression from becoming your identity. The next trap?

2. Expecting extra attention and support past the point you become reasonably whole

When you are in the middle of the long dark tunnel, the extra care and support of trusted friends and family are absolutely necessary. Recovery usually happens like this: you make forward progress, then you regress a bit. More progress occurs, and then you go backwards a little. Recovery from depression is not a straight line upward. You need propping up during this season to help you balance out these ups and downs. But once you are patched up emotionally, it's possible to subconsciously fall into the trap of expecting the same level of care and reinforcement indefinitely. This often leads to the third trap.

3. Not genuinely wanting to get well

*"Some time later, Jesus went up to Jerusalem for a feast of the Jews. Now there is in Jerusalem near the Sheep Gate a pool, which in Aramaic is called Bethesda and which is surrounded by five covered colonnades. Here a great number of disabled people used to lie—the blind, the lame, the paralyzed. One who was there had been an invalid for **thirty-eight years** [emphasis added]. When Jesus saw him lying there and learned that he had been in this condition for a long time, he asked him, "Do you want to get well?"* (John 5:1-6).

The first time I read this as a young believer I distinctly remember thinking: "What kind of question is that, Jesus? Of course this guy wants to get well. He's been unable to move on his own for thirty-eight years! Who wouldn't want to be able to walk by himself?"

Life experience is clarifying at times, is it not? I have discovered to my surprise some people grow comfortable with being sick. It bothers me to say this, but it is possible to get used to being depressed, and not really want to get well. It is a subtle snare which leaves people in a continual state of unhealthy dependency.

4. Once you are well, falling back into old habits

The choice to stay alert is crucial to your *long-term* emotional health. There is life after depression. Joy and peace do return. You get to a place where you are able to string together weeks and months of feeling good. This may be the most dangerous part of your recovery. You are feeling better. Emotional stability has re-emerged and you mistakenly let your guard down. This trap fools you into believing you can return to poor habits and still remain healthy. Nothing could be further from the truth.

Once you get to a more stable condition, dedicate yourself to learning and living the skills you will need to thrive again. Well-written, scripturally sound, research-supported books and articles are available that can help you. I have listed additional materials in the Resources Section at the end of the book. Don't try to climb out of the hole on your own. Use all of the resources at your disposal to get better.

Ten Warning Signs of Depression

Choice 5—staying alert—awakens us to the reality of recovery traps. It also keeps us aware of the warning signs of depression. In chapter one, we discovered depression is more than the inevitable sadness or disappointment coming from living in a fallen world.

Everyone has a blue day or two occasionally. What we are dealing with here involves more than experiencing a few bad days in a row.

So the question is, "How do we distinguish genuine depression from normal emotional mood shifts?" Clinical depression can be identified by a combination of five or more recognizable symptoms lasting for at least two weeks. These warning signs tend to coalesce around ten common signals we need to consider. The National Institute of Mental Health lists the following ten symptoms of depression: [1]

1. Insomnia, early-morning wakefulness, or excessive sleeping

My battle with depression included intense insomnia. I would climb into bed about 10:30 p.m., lie awake until 1:00 a.m., and finally drift off to sleep for 1-2 hours—and then be awake for the rest of the night. This pattern continued for several weeks and intensified my depressed mood.

2. Overeating or appetite loss

My experience included a significant decrease of appetite along with considerable weight loss. For others, an unusual increase in appetite may signal danger.

3. Loss of interest in activities or hobbies that once proved pleasurable, including sex

Normal daily life—work, play, time spent with family and friends—may yield little pleasure to a depressed person. At the low point of my depression and for several months afterward while recovering, my interest in sex noticeably diminished.

DEPRESSION THRIVES IN ISOLATION

A depressed person often complains of having no energy to deal with people. Therefore, they tend to isolate themselves, which usually compounds a person's distress. Depression thrives in isolation. Consequently, it is critical to surround yourself with the *right kind* of people during your battle with this affliction. Their qualifications include being loving and supportive people who are genuinely committed to you. Although they may like to, they are wise enough to avoid trying to speed up your recovery.

4. Persistent aches or pains, headaches, cramps, or digestive problems that do not ease even with treatment

In my case, I experienced phantom physical symptoms, such as numbness in my arms and legs. Neurological tests ruled out any physical explanation for those sensations. I also suffered with a persistent feeling of choking coupled with difficulty breathing. Once again, multiple visits to my family doctor and an ear-nose-throat specialist yielded no explanation. The ENT specialist suggested it could be stress-related. I found out soon after he was right.

5. Fatigue and decreased energy

At the bottom of my emotional black hole I found it difficult to accomplish much of anything. I would go into the office, knock one item off the list and find myself totally exhausted. Worse yet, I discovered helping my wife with our four young boys was problematic. Raising children requires energy and I had precious little in reserve. For a while, I even found driving a car to be emotionally draining.

6. Feelings of guilt, worthlessness, and helplessness

There were times during my struggle when it seemed like I couldn't do anything. As a task-oriented person, I felt useless and guilty. Depression feeds a sense of helplessness, coupled with the fear that life is spinning out of control.

DEPRESSION
COLORS
EVERYTHING

7. Feelings of hopelessness and pessimism

In the darkest days of my depression, a pervading sense of despair surrounded me. It was so palpable—even when the sun was shining—I would look out the window, the landscape seemed gray and gloomy. Depression colors everything. When I read John 3:16, *"For God so loved the world, that He gave His one and only*

Son, that whoever believes in Him shall not perish but have eternal life," I believed those words were true for everyone—except me.

Hopelessness often leads a depressed person to conclude her life is over. If she says those words to you, she is not being melodramatic. She is simply relaying what she believes to be true.

8. Irritability or restlessness

Clinically depressed individuals find patience elusive. It takes very little to set them off. You may notice them pacing the floor or being fidgety.

9. Persistent sad, anxious, or empty feelings

The emotional pain of depression can be overwhelming. I lost my mother to cancer when I was 23 years old. I was close to Mom, and her death was a painful blow. Oddly enough, the pain of clinical depression felt even worse.

I experienced uncontrollable crying spells for several weeks. Panic attacks were common. I even suffered several of these anxiety attacks while preaching at my church. Somehow I hid my distress, forced my way through to the end of the messages, and then escaped to my office while someone else dismissed the service in prayer.

10. Thoughts of suicide or suicide attempts

According to the National Institute of Mental Health (NIMH), as many as 90% of those who commit suicide are clinically depressed, have a substance abuse problem, or both. When I was depressed, I felt dead on the inside. I sensed no joy, no hope, and wrestled with incredibly dark thoughts. Eventually, I found myself thinking about the least painful way to take my life.

According to NIMH, if you or someone you love experiences up to five of these symptoms for more than two weeks, it's time to seek help. Make an appointment with your medical doctor immediately, and locate a competent counselor right away. Humble yourself and enlist the help you need. Surround yourself with mature, loving people who will allow you to wrestle through the experience without quoting scriptures to you or trying to cast out a demon from you. I believe in the power of the Word of God, but the last thing a clinically depressed person needs is a lecture, or spiritual clichés such as, "Let go and let God," or "If you just pray more, you'll feel better."

In chapter one I stated those who suffer with bipolar disorder or schizophrenia have options. Bipolar disorder affects approximately 5.7 million adult Americans ages 18 and older according to NIMH.[2] NIMH indicates approximately 1% of Americans suffer with schizophrenia.[3] People diagnosed with bipolar disorder or schizophrenia can manage their symptoms with proper treatment. A combination of medication and therapeutic counseling/psychotherapy is typical and often successful.

DEPRESSION IS NOT A LIFE SENTENCE

Here is the good news—*depression is not a life sentence.* If you are depressed, your life is not over. Many people with a depressive illness never seek treatment. But the majority, even those with the most severe depression, can get better with treatment.[4] Get the help you need.

Before moving on to the Epilogue, take a few moments to reflect on depression's traps and warning signs. Then speak out loud this *I-CHOOSE* statement:

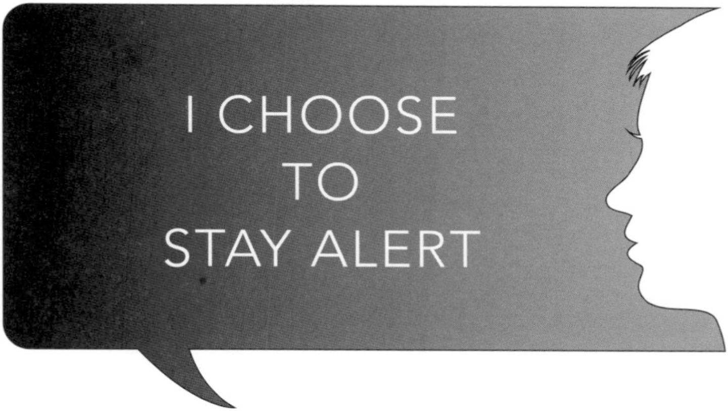
I CHOOSE
TO
STAY ALERT

EPILOGUE

My world crashed in on me in November 1992. Fast-forward five years. It was a sunny and cold December day. My best friend and I were eating breakfast at a local Big Boy restaurant.

I remember telling him the following words as if I had spoken them five minutes ago: "When the depression hit, it felt like I lost my connection with God. Prayer and Bible study actually made me feel worse for a while. The scariest part was I didn't know if God was on my side anymore. It's taken a long time—but I *know* now God really *is* for me, not against me." Tears were flowing again—only this time, they were tears of relief. Life had returned to a new normal.

Five years—if that seems like a long recovery path, you are right. The first two years involved God helping me to put myself back together mentally and emotionally. The final piece of the healing puzzle took longer—re-establishing my sense of connection with Him. I knew in theory He had not abandoned me—but it certainly felt that way.

GOD CAN PUT US BACK TOGETHER

During the recuperation period, I maintained the daily disciplines of reading the Bible and prayer (except for the first month after the initial crash). But for a long time these routines were mechanical. I did them because I knew they were right to do—but it felt like my prayers were bouncing off the ceiling and coming back to me without reaching God.

In God's providence, He moved us to a new city for work and in that area was a group of Jesus-followers that He used to complete my recovery. His presence in the meetings at this church was so powerful I could not get through a service without being in tears. Soaking in the presence of God for six months at this church proved to be the instrument He used to bring spiritual healing. He worked through this group of believers to help me regain a sense of genuine relationship with Him.

The fact that I can write this book, reasonably whole in spirit and soul, is testimony to God's ability to put us back together when we've been undone. Romans 8:28 is really true: *"And we know that in all things God works for the good of those who love him, who have been called according to his purpose."*

Healing didn't happen overnight. Could it have come about faster? Yes—and that is one of the primary purposes of this book—to shorten the recovery curve for others suffering with depression.

Don't you wish God would wave His hand over your crisis and make it instantly disappear? Most times however, His plan includes us building an entirely new approach to our lives, one brick at a time.

My recovery was a long process. It *started* with making a new choice—choosing to obey all three parts of the greatest commandment—loving God, loving my neighbor, and loving myself. Loving myself simply means thinking about, talking about, and treating myself like God does.

Loving yourself—the third part of the greatest commandment—is foundational. It is central in your quest to become unshakable. If you get this first choice right, the other four will be easier to implement. Just remember, getting it right isn't about perfection—it's about progress. The more progress you make, the more unshakable you become.

My emotional healing *continued* by unlearning old, unhealthy patterns of relating to myself and others, and choosing to adopt new, healthy, biblical habits. I sought help from competent medical professionals. I took advantage of antidepressant medications. I reworked my schedule to include more time with my family and friends. Exercise became part of my routine, and I even changed my eating habits!

It still surprises me God continues to use the most painful season of my life to bring hope and healing to others. Only He can do that. He really does make beauty out of ashes. He takes our deepest pain and transforms it into our greatest ministry, if we cooperate with Him.

Brian Dyson, President of Chatham International, made a profound statement in his 1991 commencement speech at Georgia Tech University: "Imagine life as a game in which you are juggling 5 balls in the air. You name them—work, family, health, friends, and spirit—you're keeping all of these in the air. You will soon understand that work is a rubber ball. If you drop it, it will bounce back. But the other four balls—family, health, friends and spirit—are made of glass. If you drop one of these, it will be irrevocably scuffed, marked, nicked, damaged or even shattered. It will never be the same. You must understand that."[1]

As I have stated repeatedly, one of the most subtle temptations human beings face is ignoring our family, health, friends, and spirit to pursue advancement in our career. Christians tend to spiritualize this impulse: "I'm working hard for God." Or they rationalize it: "I'm working like this so my family can have a better life." What we forget is career success means nothing if we don't have a close relationship with our family. We will not be able to enjoy the fruits of our labor if we lose our health.

THE TIME HAS COME FOR AN EMOTIONALLY HEALTHY MODEL

Success at work is less fulfilling when we have no friends to share it with. And in the end, it is a poor substitute for a growing relationship with God.

The time has come for a healthy emotional model. When you review the principles outlined in this book, you discover the pattern put forward is not new. The Scriptures clearly lay it out for us, but somewhere along the line we have lost our way. And we have paid a heavy price.

I envision a day when people live with common-sense priorities, reasonable schedules, and healthy relational boundaries. I dream of a time when Christians live with a renewed personal love for God, well-developed emotional health, and pure motivation. I long for the season when they are joyfully and productively serving in their God-given calling, and are able to do so for the long haul.

The apostle Paul concluded his second letter to Timothy with these famous words: *"I have fought the good fight, I have finished the race, I have kept the faith. Now there is in store for me a crown of righteousness, which the Lord, the righteous Judge, will award to me on that day—and not only to me, but to all who have longed for His appearing"* (2 Timothy 4:7-8).

Emotional health is available to you. Love yourself. Manage your anger. Protect yourself from abuse. Refuel emotionally. And stay alert. These five choices will help you finish your race well.

It is my sincere hope and prayer the approach sketched out in these pages will catch fire in our communities and our nation. I look forward to the day when depression rates plummet.

If you find yourself in an emotional crisis, reach out for help.

There is no shame in admitting you are human. Seek the assistance of a competent licensed therapist and your medical doctor. Do not be afraid to take advantage of medicines developed to help stabilize your brain chemistry while you work through the issues contributing to your distress.

GIVE TO YOURSELF EMOTIONALLY

Learn how to give to yourself emotionally. Remember God is more interested in you as a person than He is in your career, your bank account, or your achievements.

You can have a better life—more enjoyable relationships with people—and greater stability in a chaotic world. I hope you choose to become unshakable. Be intentional about the Five Choices:

I CHOOSE TO LOVE MYSELF AS JESUS COMMANDED.

I CHOOSE TO MANAGE MY ANGER INSTEAD OF IT MANAGING ME.

I CHOOSE TO PROTECT MYSELF FROM ABUSIVE PEOPLE.

I CHOOSE TO REFUEL EMOTIONALLY.

I CHOOSE TO STAY ALERT.

I'm rooting and praying for you!
John Opalewski

NOTES

INTRODUCTION

1. Joshua Wolf Schenk, *Lincoln's Great Depression*, October 2005, The Atlantic.

2. www.nimn.nih.gov

3. Ibid.

4. Elizabeth Sherrill, used by permission.

CHAPTER FOUR

1. Norman Vincent Peale, *The Power of Positive Thinking*, 1952, Simon & Schuster.

2. Wayne Cordeiro, *Leading on Empty*, 2010, Bethany House Publishers.

3. Ibid.

4. From HBR blog, *"The Magic of Doing One Thing at a Time"* by Tony Schwartz, www.hbr.org, March 2012.

5. Wayne Cordeiro, *Leading on Empty*, 2010, Bethany House Publishers.

CHAPTER FIVE

1. www.nimh.nih.gov

2. Ibid.

3. Ibid.

4. Ibid.

EPILOGUE

1. Brian Dyson, *Commencement Speech at Georgia Tech University,* 1991, used by permission.

ADDITIONAL RESOURCES FROM CONVERGE COACHING

TAKE CHARGE OF YOUR MENTAL & EMOTIONAL HEALTH
John Opalewski

Learn how to take ownership of your mental and emotional health. This four-part series—available in DVD and CD formats—offers practical help and hope to those suffering with depression. It equips emotionally healthy people to stay well-adjusted, while effectively helping those in depression's grip.

Pick up a copy today at www.convergecoach.com

MONSTERS IN THE CLOSET
John Opalewski

Fear and anxiety are the enemies of joy and peace. Christians are not immune to the control of fear and anxiety. These twin adversaries can cause us to retreat, hoard, lie, underachieve, over-medicate, or act out. This four-part series—available in CD format—details practical strategies for living productively in the face of fear.

Pick up a copy today at www.convergecoach.com

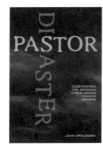

PASTOR DISASTER
CONFRONTING THE GROWING CRISIS
AMONG CHURCH LEADERS
John Opalewski

Pastoring a church can be hazardous to a leader's health. Difficult people, dysfunctional families, unrealistic expectations, and spiritual warfare present challenges to a pastor's longevity and health. More than 1,000 pastors leave the ministry every month due to burnout, contention in their church, or moral failure. Their exodus has contributed to the decline of the Church's impact on Western culture.

The question is . . . what can we do? How can leaders lead longer and better? This practical guide, written for pastors, leaders, and churchgoers, identifies the real problems behind the current leadership crisis. It provides workable solutions to strengthen leaders and help the Church re-establish its influence.

Pick up a copy today at www.convergecoach.com

E-book available on iPad, Kindle, Nook, Kobo, Copia and many other platforms

ABOUT THE AUTHOR

John Opalewski graduated from Oral Roberts University and served as a pastor for 15 years. He is a certified Coach with Natural Church Development (NCD). For the past 20 years, John has also worked in the Information Technology industry. He currently holds certifications as a VMware TSP (Technical Sales Professional); EMC-VSC (Velocity Systems Engineer); NetApp AIP (Accredited Installation Professional); NCDA (NetApp Certified Data Management Administrator); and NASAP (NetApp Accredited Storage Architect Professional).

John's experience as a leader in both the church and business arenas has made him a sought-after international speaker, consultant, and mentor. He and his wife, Laura, have been married more than 30 years and have four sons. Together they founded Converge Coaching, LLC in 2012 to help leaders be effective in their roles while maintaining health in their personal lives.

CONTACT AND ORDERING INFORMATION

Additional books available for purchase through our website: www.convergecoach.com

Bulk discounts available

eBook platforms also available:
- Amazon Kindle
- Barnes & Noble (Nook)
- iBookstore
- Sony
- Kobo
- Copia
- Gardners
- Baker & Taylor
- eBookPie

For more information about other resources and services available through Converge Coaching, LLC, please visit our website: www.convergecoach.com

Contact John at: john@convergecoach.com

·